Emma Tennant spent her childhood in Scotland. She has a son and two daughters, and lives in west London. Her novels include *The Colour of Rain*, *The Adventures of Robina*, *Black Marina*, *The Crack*, *Hotel De Dream*, *The Last of the Country House Murders*, *The Bad Sister*, *Two Women of London* and *Faustine*.

THE

Of Writing

Emma Tennant

faber and faber

LONDON · BOSTON

First published in 1992
by Faber and Faber Limited
3 Queen Square London WC1N 3AU

Photoset by Parker Typesetting Service, Leicester
Printed in Great Britain by
Clays Ltd, St Ives plc

Thanks to the following for contributions and suggestions:
Tim Owens; Michael Neve; Peter Wollen; Hilary Bailey;
Christopher Hawtree

A CIP record for this book is
available from the British Library

ISBN 0-571-16966-X

Accidie

'The malady of monks, that deadly weakness
of the will that is the root of all evil.'

Charles Baudelaire

Ackroyd

(v.t.) To take long past events, preferably
murky, and link them with later, unexpected
consequences, and trust to luck to produce a
novel. Such productions invariably come with
a brown-hued wrapper across which is strewn
a collage of statues, sepia prints and old maps.

Advance

The sum of money offered by the publisher in
return for a book and placed against royalties.
The size of the advance is often in inverse
proportion to the girth of the publisher, i.e. a
large, generously endowed publisher is liable
to offer an impossibly stingy amount, while
fortunes have been handed out by a Slim Jim
or a Beanpole Bob. (The writer should also be
able to gauge the probable size of the advance
by the type of meal at which the book is dis-
cussed. Again, size is in inverse ratio to the

noughts at the end of the figure, a half-mouthful of marinated salmon and a sliced fig portending more than a hearty meat-and-two-veg.) See **Lunch**.

Advertising

Literature's Big Brother.

Alcohol

The writer's wicked stepmother – offering the poisoned apple of fame and success which plunges its victim into a seven-year coma. See **Hangover**.

Allegory

A fairy-tale with a hidden political meaning. State repression (i.e. olden-times USSR or Eastern Bloc) is needed for the genre to thrive and capitalism is not generally considered menacing enough to justify the metamorphosis required (characters as beasts, magical beings, etc.) – though the allegory can be detected today in unexpected forms (see **Gothic**). The most famous example of everyone missing the point of an allegory is *Animal Farm* by George

Orwell, which the Right took as a savage attack on Stalin's Communism and the Left took as a swingeing attack on capitalist values.

Anecdote

Narrative of a detached incident. Too many years of telling such incidents lead to anecdotage – a state of garrulous old age in which nobody listens to you any longer.

Aphorism

1 A novelistic time-span reduced to an instant. Boswell describes Dr Johnson prophesying that all writing, grown 'weary of preparation, and connection, and illustration, and all those arts by which a big book is made', will eventually become aphoristic.

2 'The great writers of aphorisms read as though they had all known each other very well.'

Elias Canetti

Apprenticeship

'Learn to write well, or not to write at all.'

John Dryden

Auction

In the heady days of boom several publishers would be invited to bid for the same book, or even a book that had not yet been written (see Pirandello's *Six Synopses in Search of an Author*, a satirical work showing the confusion of both writer and publisher and their interchangeable identities at the time of auction). Represents the triumph of the Deal over the Spiel, and is followed by an occasion of celebration or commiseration (see **Lunch**).

Audience

1 'Ideally, the writer needs no audience other than the few who understand. It is immodest and greedy to want more. Unhappily, the novelist, by the very nature of his coarse art, is greedy and immodest; unless he is read by everyone he cannot delight, instruct, reform, destroy a world he wants, at the least, to be different for his having lived in it.'

Gore Vidal

2 'The literary man has a circle of the chosen who read him and become his only public. What more natural, then, that he should write for those who, even if they do not pay

him, at least understand him?'

Amado Nervo

Author

1 A writer suffering from severe constipation.

2 'A man may be a very good author with some faults, but not with many faults.'

Voltaire

3 'We are only the actors, we are never wholly the authors of our own deeds or works.'

D. H. Lawrence

Author's Wife

Must understand that her family circle includes a frail, crotchety relative – who is nevertheless more interesting and alluring than her. See also **Literary Widows**.

Autobiography

'My principal objection wasn't the *vanity* involved in writing one's autobiography. Such books are like all others: quickly forgotten if boring. What I was frightened of was deflowering the happy moments I've experienced by describing and dissecting them.'

Stendhal

Automatic Writing

The furthest stage of the male writer's exploitation of his wife. Prime example is Mrs W. B. Yeats, forced to sit all night holding a pen while the spirits 'dictated' and her mind raced across the page (Yeats slept). The result: unreadable. Not recommended.

Avant Garde

Obs. (See **Isms**.) A 'movement' led by a small coterie with ideas for changing the world. The concept of the Avant Garde actually arose when the world was going through huge technological changes and a scientific revolution overtook the Industrial Revolution. It was important for each movement to spell out its beliefs and artistic rules. See **Manifesto**.

B

Barbara Cartland

Novel. Goy meets girl.

Bias

'The novelist is at the mercy of his bias. The subjects he chooses, the character he invents and his attitude towards them is conditioned by it. He loads the dice.'

W. Somerset Maugham

Bibliophile

'Has approximately the same relationship to literature as a philatelist to geography.'

Karl Kraus

Big Men's Books

Must contain EMPIRE, GOD, RULER, WORLD, WAR in the title.

Big Women's Books

Women readers are expected to have a sense of history spanning three generations only:

grandmother, mother and daughter figure at mind-numbing length.

Biography

Muesli for the middle-aged.

Block

A total inability on the part of the writer to put pen to paper. (The affliction is not solved by relying on machines: see **Word Processor**.) Solution for the new writer: try another profession. Block – which, if intoned often enough takes on the persona of an ancient Indian god – can ruin the purse and the health; and can descend suddenly, even on the most practised of writers.

Blockbuster

Mentally deficient heir of Trollope, Dickens, George Eliot, etc.

Bloomsbury Group

Started as a small business thirty years ago by Michael Holroyd selling 'Strachey', its turnover became enormous by the mid-80s and still shows little sign of decline, with new lines in 'Woolf' still commissioned and branches specializing in 'Carrington', 'Grant' and 'Bell' opening in the most remote provincial areas. Wide appeal.

Boasting

'The author who speaks about his own books is as bad as the mother who talks about her children.'

Benjamin Disraeli

Book

1 'I think a writer writes only one book, although that same book may appear in several volumes, under different titles. You see it with Balzac, Conrad, Melville, Kafka, and of course with Faulkner. One of these books sometimes stands out far above the rest so that the writer seems to be the author of a single, primordial work.'

Gabriel Garcia Marquez

2 ' "Everybody can write one good book" is one of the most idiotic sayings imaginable. It

is not even true that everybody has the material for one good book or even for one good article, for "material" is not what has happened to you but the effect upon you of what happened.'

William Plomer

3 'It seems to me that one should only read books which bite and sting one. If the book we are reading does not wake us up with a blow to the head, what's the point in reading? . . . A book must be the axe which smashes the frozen sea within us.'

Franz Kafka

Book Chain

Sells books published within the past three months at the most; stores and merchandise interchangeable.

Book Clubs

A price all can afford for a book nobody wants.

Booker Prize

1 A TV occasion of nobs and minor mafiosi. See **Prizes**.
2 Winner is guaranteed an obituary.
3 Menu: Devilled Spleen
         Pastiche Salza Victoriana
         Bone People

Bookseller

The most powerful cog in the publishing machine (see **Player**). Occasionally, schlock-busting manuscripts are sent to booksellers before the publisher decides whether or not to go ahead with the book. (Even more occasionally, the publisher has the skill, foolhardiness or integrity to make decisions for himself.) The result of this nefarious practice: a Nation of Schlockmakers.

Bores

'For a novelist they are of all people the most rewarding. Under their indigestible crust are pressed the rich and jellied delicacies of the human comedy.'

V. S. Pritchett

Brat Pack

Baby alligators come up from the sewers of New York into the bathrooms of wealthy media folk. Cutely named 'Jay' or 'Tana', they last only a few seasons before, bloated from hype and colossal advances, they are thrown back again.

Brechtian

Anything 'social-realist' in tone, deriving from the dramas written by the women – Elisabeth Hauptmann, Helene Weigel, Ruth Berlau, etc. – who together made up the writer known as Brecht.

Bursary

Only unprincipled authors turn them down.

Calf-Bound Volume

Presentation copy (or consolation prize) given to runner-up for a literary award (see **Prizes**) of his or her own novel – the last thing he or she wants to see instead of a cheque and lasting fame. Increasingly, the calf-bound volume is becoming an endangered species: animal rights activists will put an end to the custom.

Canon

1 A group of texts which none of us wants to read from beginning to end. The traditional canon was painstakingly constructed to honour the substantial works of great white males which had stood the test of time and demonstrated their transcendent value to the most stringent of white male critics. In time, of course, the clubable consensus was exploded and the canon opened up to new waves of contemporary, feminist, multi-cultural and insurgent texts. Unfortunately each new wave admitted meant heaving out somebody's old favourite, until the canon began to lose any semblance of logic or consistency. As a result, critical opinion divided into three schools: Reactionaries, who loudly

called for the old canon to be reinstated; Radicals, who felt that the canon should become a maelstrom of manouevre and contention; and Sceptics, who believed the time had come for the canon to be discharged.

2 'If one is in doubt as to the merit of a writer, the best course one can take is to make him, so to speak, run the gauntlet of the "great masters". We must '"lodge well in our minds" lines and expressions of the great masters – "short passages, even single lines will serve our turn quite sufficiently" – and these we shall find an "infallible touchstone" for testing the value of all other poetry. The plan is delightfully simple; there is, indeed, only one small difficulty about it: it cannot come into operation until we have decided the very question which it is intended to solve – namely, who "the great masters" are.'

Lytton Strachey (on Matthew Arnold)

Censorship

1 A great deal of it about – see the periodical *Index on Censorship*. Since the heady days of Lady Chatterley (see **Porn**), there has been no censorship to speak of in England or the US,

with the famous exception of the scandalous pronouncement of a death sentence by the Ayatollah Khomeini on Salman Rushdie.

2 'If censorship reigns there cannot be sincere flattery, and only small men are afraid of small writing.'

Pierre de Beaumarchais

Chat Show

A writer Bragging is a fearsome sight.

Chattering Classes

A British expression of contempt for those who think. Intellectuals – a dirty word – are envisaged with a (faded) hammer and sickle in one hand and a glass of champagne in the other.

Classic

1 'Who lasts a century can have no flaw,
   I hold that Wit a Classic, good in law.'

Alexander Pope

2 'A work of art which does not modify our life in any way, which does not remain in

some corner of our memory (even though transformed and disguised), does not exist for us. It is not a living work. But the art of the past has already been sifted: for the art of today we, its contemporaries, form the first sieve, the first experimenters. Let us give the big fish time to remain in the net and the little fish time to slip through the holes. Let us give memory time to perform its first and most urgent task: to forget.'

Eugenio Montale

3 'When you re-read a classic you do not see more in the book than you did before; you see more in *you* than you did before.'

Clifton Fadiman

4 **Classic, twentieth-century.** A desperate attempt on the part of a publisher to lend dignity and instant respectability to a forgotten novel. Method of storage: varnish and keep in a cool place.

Companionship

'Choose an author as you choose a friend.'

Wentworth Dillon

Concept

Hollywood-ese for an idea which, if successful, will result in the pronouncement 'We
have a movie!' Concepts should be High (e.g.
'Woman marries two men; they bond; she
marries a third') or 'Fish Out of Water' (e.g.
'Waiter in a greasy spoon turns out to be
Crown Prince of Romania'). They should on
no account be Low (Danish boy grows up on
nineteenth-century farm, nothing happens)
unless they are directed by a relative of
Ingmar Bergman.

Concision

1 'The point of good writing is knowing when
to stop.'

L. M. Montgomery

2 'The writer does the most, who gives his
reader the most knowledge, and takes from
him the least time.'

C. C. Colton

Conglomerates

Big publishing groups only interested in the
Princess of Whales.

Contemporaries

'The great works of past ages seem to a young man things of another race in respect to which his faculties must remain passive and submiss, even as to the stars and mountains. But the writings of a contemporary, perhaps not many years older than himself, surrounded by the same circumstances and disciplined by the same manners, possess a *reality* for him and inspire an actual friendship as of a man for a man.'

S. T. Coleridge

Copy Editor

Complete stranger who rewrites your book to suit his/her own ideas and changes the position of every comma.

Copyright

On works published during the author's lifetime, copyright lapses fifty years from the end of the year of the author's death – and not, as an advertising company selling Irish whiskey with James Joyce copy recently found to its cost, fifty years from date of publication.

Cover

'Embossed in gold/One million copies sold.'
(Old English)

Creative Writing Course

The unreadable in pursuit of the unteachable.

Creativity

1 'A man should begin to write soon; for, if he waits till his judgement is matured, his inability, through want of practice to express his conceptions, will make the disproportion so great between what he sees and what he can attain, that he will probably be discouraged from writing at all.'

Samuel Johnson

2 'I have little patience with the "creative reader".'

William Gass

Critic

1 'What a dull and dreary trade is that of critic. It is so difficult to create a thin, even a mediocre

thing; it is so easy to detect mediocrity.'

Denis Diderot

2 'You know who the critics are? The men who have failed in literature and art.'

Benjamin Disraeli

Criticism

'Criticism, by itself, does nothing and can do nothing. The best of it can act only in concert, and almost in collaboration, with public feeling. I shall venture to say that the critic is only the secretary of the public – though a secretary who does not wait to be dictated to, but each morning divines and redacts the general opinion. Even when he has actually expressed the thought which everybody has (or would like to have), a great and living part of his allusions, of his conclusions, and of their consequences, remains in the wits of his readers. I maintain that in reading over old papers and their most successful critiques we never find more than half the article in print – the other was written only in the reader's mind. You are to suppose a sheet printed of which we only read one side – the other has disappeared, is blank.'

Sainte-Beuve

Cult Novel

Usually SF or something stranger: addicts of the cult novel have been known to stalk the writer late at night in his home and demand further supplies. In the case of J. D. Salinger, this approach proved non-productive.

Cutting Edge

Writers said to be on the cutting edge are male and would need a haircut if it weren't for the obvious recent loss.

Dead White English Males

Responsible for the wave of disapproval and puritanism at present sweeping campuses in the West. See **Politically Correct**.

Dead Writers

'Someone said: "The dead writers are remote from us because we *know* so much more than they did." Precisely, and because they are that which we know.'

Cyril Connolly

Decadence

'To live in a decadence need not make us despair; it is but one technical problem the more which a writer has to solve.'

Cyril Connolly

Decency

'Literary men are the children of their age, and so like all the rest of the lot must subordinate themselves to external conditions of living together. They must be absolutely decent.'

Anton Chekhov

Deconstruction

'What I've just said could be the opposite of what you think I've just said, or the opposite of what I've just said.'

Delivery Date

Only the guilty writer delivers on time.

Desire

'Desire is the great enemy of the novelist. How when he is describing his hero or heroine is he to resist the intoxicating temptation of projecting his sexual wishes? When he describes love affairs how is he to avoid becoming secretly involved? The amorous struggle at the desk is a comical and humiliating episode in the life of the novelist; the best sellers, who do not struggle but let everything rip, look back upon him with vacuous pity.'

V. S. Pritchett

Despair

'One must work, if not from inclination at least from despair, since, as I have fully proved, to work is less wearisome than to amuse oneself.'

Charles Baudelaire

Dictionary

'To find a tongue one has to be an academician – deader than a fossil – to make a dictionary of any language at all!'

Arthur Rimbaud

Discovered Writer

Usually female, photographed with knitting wool in remote and unsanitary cottage. A gruff female companion is an optional extra. This specimen of writer dies soon after being 'discovered' by eminent literati: the train journeys to London and champagne from publishers accustomed to show little respect (see **Pulp**) quickly prove too much for her. The demise results in an unexpected windfall for nephews and nieces previously unaware of the existence of a literary figure in the family (see **Estate**).

Discovery

'To a man with an ear for verbal delicacies, the man who searches painfully for the perfect word, and puts the way of saying things above the thing said – there is in writing the constant joy of sudden discovery, of happy accident.'

H. L. Mencken

Diseases

1 'Against the disease of writing one must take special precautions, since it is a dangerous and contagious disease.'

Peter Abelard

2 'There are two literary maladies – writer's cramp and swollen head. The worst of writer's cramp is that it is never cured; the worst of swollen head is that it never kills.'

Coulson Kernahan

Disillusion

'When all is said and done, Art is perhaps no more serious than a game of ninepins. Perhaps everything is an immense bluff. I am afraid of that. And when we turn the page we may be very surprised to find that the answer to the riddle is so simple.'

Gustave Flaubert

Dissident

Once an escapee from Communism, prized and fêted in the West, now a vanished species. Western poets who used to complain that there were more readers per refusenik than they could get hot dinners now confront the fact that world capitalism has made them all brothers under the skin. There are still plenty of dissidents, of course, those writers who live in oppressive regimes the world over. But they have never had the glamour 'dissident' treatment, perhaps because, if they were allowed a choice at all, they'd rather be Re(a)d than Dead.

Doorstopper

1 Joke or slang word to describe a large book or tome.

2 'The composition of vast books is a laborious and impoverishing extravagance. To go for five hundred pages developing an idea

whose perfect oral exposition is possible in a few minutes! A better course of action is to pretend that these books already exist, and then to offer a resumé, a commentary.'

Jorge Luis Borges

Dress

'The first thing a novelist has to learn is self-effacement – that first and that always. Not for him the flowing locks, sombreros, flaming ties, eccentric pants. If he gets himself up like a poet, humanity will act towards him as if he were a poet – disagreeably.'

Ford Madox Ford

Drug

'A losing trade, I assure you, sire: literature is a drug.'

George Borrow

Editor

Fails to read mss. Moves frequently, sometimes stuffing a few selling authors in a suitcase on the way.

Education

'We shouldn't teach great books; we should teach a love of reading.'

Burrhus Frederic Skinner

Elite

The literary world is suspected of every vice, the worst being élitism. Members of this group are distinguished from the rest of the world by the hugeness of their reviews and the veil drawn over the size of their advances – many of which have been procured for them by the new Lady of the Manor of **Sissinghurst**.

El Vino's

Well-known London urinal frequented by hacks, where, by tradition, the men pee sitting down and the women standing up.

Empire Novel

Dying breed, dealing in colonial guilt.

Employment

'With the exception of one extraordinary man I have never known an individual, least of all an individual of genius, healthy or happy without a profession, i.e. some regular employment, which does not depend on the will of the moment, and which can be carried on so far mechanically that an average quantum only of health, spirits and intellectual exertion are requisite to its faithful discharge.'

S. T. Coleridge

Enemies

1 'Enemies of deep new art: The history of art. Courses in comparative literature. Courses in creative writing. The history of ideas. Prizes. Performing authors.'

Geoffrey Grigson

2 **Enemies of Promise.** The title of Cyril Connolly's autobiography. 'It is necessary now to analyse the conditions which govern the high rate of mortality among contem-

porary writers, to enter a region "where the thin harvest waves its wither'd ears . . . a sombre, but to those for whom it is not yet too late, a bracing territory".' Taking the weeds on Crabbe's heath as symbols, Connolly defines journalism as the Blue Bugloss: 'by degrees the flippancy of journalism will become a habit'; the Slimy Mallow represents worldly success, the Charlock is 'sex with its obsessions', and the 'clasping tares' are the ties of duty and domesticity, 'blights from which no writer is immune'.

English Language

1 'The English language is like a broad river on whose bank a few patient anglers are sitting, while, higher up, the stream is being polluted by a string of refuse-barges tipping out their muck.'

Cyril Connolly

2 'From the odd prose that he writes I suspect that his first language is not English.'

Gore Vidal (on Frederick Forsyth)

Estate

The royalties and books, unpublished and published, of a dead writer – who often makes one last spiteful move by appointing an unsuspecting ex-friend or relative an Executor. Duties in administering an Estate can be boundless – from giving permission for a musical to refusing an 'investigative' journalist the right to reprint portions of the dead author's work, in the vain hope that the biography will remain unwritten and scurrilous details will not be dragged out of the closet.

Epistolary Novel

The fax cannot replace Richardson or Laclos. Lacking all privacy, it cannot produce the missive that is slipped under the carpet (*Tess of the d'Urbervilles*) or pushed down the bosom of the wicked Marquise de Merteuil – proving that the envelope is worth more than the letter it contains.

Ethnic Writer

Encouraged by publishers with an eye on a Big Prize. Must be prepared to write about the

ruins of Empire and about far-distant places –
or, at the very least, about families with cus-
toms that have the allure of the exotic for the
standard British reader. Seldom paid much for
their efforts (see **Advance**) but, if the gamble
pays off, the EW may find him- or herself on
year-round trips in luxury air-conditioned circumstances to the far-flung destinations described so painstakingly in the prize-winning
tome (see **Freebie**).

Fable

Popular after years of neglect, the fable is more accessible to a wide ethnic and social mix than the mainstream novel: there is no problem with domestic details, religious practices, etc., as the fable is, like a fairy-tale, understandable by all. It does, however, lack **Irony**, the dry-Martini-with-olive of Western culture. Note: do not attempt to be fabulous if you are a Professor of English. No one will believe you.

Failure

'Failure is infectious. The world is full of charming failures (for all charming people have something to conceal, usually their total dependence on the appreciation of others) and unless a writer is quite ruthless with these amiable footlers, they will drag him down with them.'

Cyril Connolly

Fairy-Tale

A life with a happy ending. Grimm.

Fame

1 'It is advantageous to an author, that his book should be attacked as well as praised. Fame is a shuttlecock. If it be struck at only one end of the room, it will soon fall to the ground. To keep it up, it must be struck at both ends.'

Samuel Johnson

2 'Quite often in society I used to come across people who would congratulate me on one of my works: I'd written very few then. The compliment and my reply done with, we didn't know what to say to each other. These Parisians, who expected some frivolously pat reply, must have thought me very gauche, and perhaps very proud.'

Stendhal

3 '*One Hundred Years of Solitude* nearly ruined my life. Nothing was ever the same again after it was published. Because fame unsettles your sense of reality, almost as much as power, perhaps, and it continually threatens your private life.'

Gabriel Garcia Marquez

4 'By the way, being an eminent author is not so great a delight. For one thing, it's a gloomy

life. Work from morning to night, and not much sense to it. Money – as scarce as hen's teeth.'

Anton Chekhov

5 'Nothing will ever match the distracted gaze of the woman serving in the butcher's who has seen you on television.'

Jean Baudrillard

Fantasy

A much sneered-at genre, suggesting whimsical yearnings, Peter Pan and the **Heritage** tradition – where a well-known American literary agent, infatuated with nostalgia, is known to dress as Virginia Woolf on summer weekends in the English countryside (see **Sissinghurst**).

More recently, Fantasy has become a genre catering to aficionados of 'Sword and Sorcery': mythical monsters battle with Sir Gawain. In Europe and Russia fantasy is taken extremely seriously as a way of showing the absurdity of the human condition.

Advice to the writer: do not try this unless you are a South American or East European.

Fiction

'Fiction has traditionally and characteristically borrowed its form from letters, journals, diaries, autobiographies, histories, travelogues, news stories, backyard gossip etc. It has simply *pretended* to be one or other of them.'

William Gass

Films

'Most best-selling books reflect to some degree the films each author saw in his formative years . . . They connect not at all with other books, but with the movies.'

Gore Vidal

Flashback

Do people really remember in sepia? Or in black and white, to slushy music? The great trickster Vladimir Nabokov informs us that the colour of memory is magenta or heliotrope, a colour that runs through the novels of Marcel Proust.

Fowler

'If I had a writer-enemy whom I wished to destroy utterly, I should give him a copy of Fowler and make him read it carefully. The chances are that his style would never recover. Fowler's chief gift is to make all his most crabbed prejudices sound like the natural beliefs of every civilised and literate man.'

Nigel Balchin

Frankfurt

Versailles for publishers. Those who fail to make a mark in the power-aisles are banished indefinitely to the provinces.

Freebie

Expenses-paid jaunt for academics and the occasional writer. The latter should beware: freebies are infiltrated by satirists disguised as professors of English literature, and the innocent writer may find an uncomfortably accurate portrayal of his or her most undesirable personal characteristics.

Frustration

'I want to cut my throat when I think that I shall never write the way I want, or set down a quarter of what I dream. All this energy we feel ourselves choking on: we are fated to die with it still in us, unexpended. It is like those sudden cravings for a lay. In imagination we lift up every passing skirt; but after the fifth discharge no sperm is left. Blood comes to the glans, but our lust is confined to our hearts.'

Gustave Flaubert

G

Garret

A perch for an impecunious young writer. Now non-existent due to property prices and high rents, forcing the aspiring writer to live at home (see **Parricide**).

Genius

'Genius is of two kinds, one of which blazes up in youth and dies down, while the other matures, like Milton's or Goethe's, through long choosing, putting out new branches every seven years.'

Cyril Connolly

Ghost

A hack who 'writes' the autobiography of a celebrity. The prose is seldom haunting.

Glory

'Achilles exists only through Homer. Take away the art of writing from this world and you will probably take away its glory.'

F. René de Chateaubriand

Good Books

'The reason why so few good books are written is that so few people who can write know anything.'

Walter Bagehot

Good Read

Used to describe something considered shameful – an illicit pleasure such as lying in bed all afternoon eating peppermint creams. The writer must be a bad writer in order for the read to be good.

Good Writing

'All good writing is swimming under water and holding your breath.'

F. Scott Fitzgerald

Gothic

First sent up by Jane Austen in *Northanger Abbey*, this has blossomed – or degenerated – into a successful genre. Gothic novels are, of course, also allegories for the painful lives of writers, who give all their blood to the publishers (see **Vampire**) in return for a tiny percentage of oxygen (see **Grub Street**) while the harmless bats and other nocturnal animals which sleep all day and party wildly at night on their cut from royalties are clearly identifiable as the authors' representatives (see **Literary Agent**).

Huge sums, however, can be made from Gothic, should the formula be got right, though – an important proviso – the author must beware the inevitable consequences of formula writing, i.e. becoming indistinguishable from other writers and therefore invisible.

Grant

A small sum of money given to a writer by a worthy body of literature-lovers, many of whom live resolutely in the past (see **Heritage**; **Bloomsbury Group**) and actually believe that the gentle work they are subsidizing has a chance of survival in the big, cruel world (see **Bookseller**; **Usp**).

Granta

An upmarket version of *Men Only*, in which macho occupations such as Travel in War-Torn Countries alternate with Third World Porn: photographs of the sick, the starving and those dying of Aids.

Greatness

1 'It is only a moment here and a moment there that the greatest writer has.'

Robert Frost

2 'No great work, or worthy of praise or memory, but came out of poor cradles.'

Ben Jonson

Grub Street

'Having no profession, he became by necessity an author.' – Dr Johnson on the bereft, dissipated Richard Savage, who, 'without lodging and meat', made up his speeches while tramping the fields or the streets, and had to beg the loan of pen and ink to scribble them on scraps paper he had picked up.

Gulag

Where serious-minded Russians go to write their novels.

Gushing

'Talking is a hydrant in the yard and writing is a faucet upstairs in the house. Opening the first takes all the pressure off the second.'

Robert Frost

Habits

1 'Curious what we remember of particular poets, I mean of their lives. I remember of Kuo Mo-jo that at twelve years old, after P.T. had been introduced from the West into Chinese schools, he discovered the pleasures of masturbation from having to climb bamboo poles, the pole between his legs.

Christina Rossetti writes her poems out in her bedroom, on the edge of the washstand. Christina Rossetti dreams of released canaries flying in a golden shower over London.

Yeats looks respectfully at Yeats reflected in the mirrors as he comes down, no as he *descends*, the staircase of the Savile Club. I've watched him.

A. E. Houseman: he reads *Ulysses* and *Lady Chatterley's Lover*, honest man, in search of kicks.

Coleridge's full bladder forces him out of bed: "What a beautiful thing urine is, in a pot, brown yellow, transpicuous, the image, diamond shaped, of the candle in it, especially, as it now appeared, I having emptied the snuffers into it, and the snuff floating about, and painting all-shaped shadows in the bottom."'

Geoffrey Grigson

2 'Never again do I want to read that he writes in longhand with a hard pencil while standing at a lectern until he tires and sits or lies down, that he writes on Bristol cards which are lined only on one side so that he will not mistake a used card for a fresh card. Reading and re-reading these descriptions, one understands why he thinks Robbe-Grillet a great writer.'

Gore Vidal, on re-reading the
interviews with Nabokov

Haiku

Slivers of raw, marinated fish which fail to satisfy the greedy appetites of the West.

Hangover

Few writers have achieved true inspiration on mineral water. The hangover is the best time to write: the world looks jaded and it is impossible to make sense of the morning's bank statement.

Happiness

'The only happy author in the world is he who is below the care of reputation.'

Washington Irving

Hardback

The appendix of the Book Trade – can be removed without anyone noticing.

Heritage

Britain's most popular literary form. Mrs Tiggywinkle is known intimately – on china mugs, soap-dishes, etc. – and is confused with Vita Sackville-West only by foreigners (see **Sissinghurst**).

Highbrow

Totally out of use. A term used freely in the Thirties and in postwar years to denote a member of a small élite who could understand Wittgenstein and was at home in the cultures of France, Germany, England and Italy. Real snobs, however, hung back from using the word, as it was considered rather common – as was, of course, the growing mass culture they would give anything to avoid. See **Middlebrow; Lowbrow**.

Historical Context

'The great poet, in writing himself, writes his time.'

T. S. Eliot

Historical Novel

Bodice-Ripper for the Blue Rinse: a Saga of Vastacres, complete with degenerate aristocratic squire with a lacy or frilly name. Must contain the line 'Oh, but she was wanton.'

History

'It takes a great deal of history to produce a little literature.'

Henry James

Honesty

'If you give me six lines written by the hand of the most honest man I will find something in them which will hang him.'

Cardinal Richelieu

Hot Water

'There is a small steam engine in his brain which not only sets the cerebral mass in motion, but keeps the owner in hot water.'

Editorial comment in New York
on Edgar Allan Poe

Hubris

No change over the past few millennia. A writer who says in interview 'I was the only young woman likely to break into Cape, which is seen as a very literary, high-class list. I thought, if I'm there it changes people's idea of what good writing is, however subtly. What I'm doing is about art but it's also about politics' (Jeanette Winterson, *Guardian*, 26/8/92) is likely already to have lost her talent and – 'unless I take to gambling in Las Vegas it's very unlikely I'll be poor again' (ibid) – will, in all probability lose the money too. A writer should always beware of tempting the Fates in this way.

Imagery

'Sometimes it crosses my mind that the things I write here are nothing other than the images that prisoners or sailors tattoo on their skins.'

George Seferis

Imagination

1 'In the world of words, the imagination is one of the forces of nature.'

Wallace Stevens

2 'Could a rule be given from without poetry would cease to be poetry and sink into a mechanical art ... The rules of the imagination are themselves the very powers of growth and production.'

S. T. Coleridge

3 'It is the fashion of the day to lay great stress upon what they call "imagination" and "invention", the two commonest of qualities: an Irish peasant with a little whisky in his head will imagine and invent more than would furnish forth a modern poem.'

Byron

Impersonality

'The progress of an artist is a continual self-sacrifice, a continual extinction of personality.'

T. S. Eliot

Improvement Books

Improvement books (gardening; cookery; diet) transport readers to the land of cockaigne, where the milk never boils over and the cat is never sick and the lawn is never churned up by kids on bicycles. Hugely popular and profitable for the publisher.

Independent Booksellers

Dying species consisting of people who like books rather than 'product'; some are preserved like Beatrix Potter, as an 'experience'.

Inner Space

J. G. Ballard forsook the explorations and adventures of Outer Space and instead wrote wild, poetic visions of the demented and tortured mind. A Sixties phenomenon. The other brilliant Inner Spaceman was R. D. Laing, with *The Self and Others* and *The Divided Self*. LSD for intellectuals.

Inspiration

'Inspiration always comes when a man wills it, but it does not always depart when he wishes.'

Charles Baudelaire

Interview

'Alas, the interview as it is generally practised has nothing to do with a dialogue: (1) the interviewer asks questions of interest to him, of no interest to you; (2) of your responses, he uses only those that suit him; (3) he translates them into his own vocabulary, his own manner of thought. In imitation of American journalism, he will not even deign to get your approval for what he has you say. The interview appears. You console yourself: people will quickly forget it! Not at all: people will quote it! Even the most scrupulous academics no longer distinguish between the words a writer has written and signed, and his remarks as reported.'

Milan Kundera

Irony

1 'An irony has no point unless it is true, in some degree, in both senses; for it is imagined as part of an argument; what is said is made absurd, but it is what the opponents might say.'

William Empson

2 'Which is right and which is wrong? Is Emma Bovary intolerable? Or brave and touching? And what about Werther? Is he sensitive and noble? Or an aggressive sentimentalist, infatuated with himself? The more attentively we read a novel, the more impossible the answer, because the novel is, by definition, the ironic art: its "truth" is concealed, undeclared, undeclarable.'

Milan Kundera

Isms

The symbols of unease and self-consciousness of the twentieth century, now thankfully drawing to a close. To match the Fascism and Communism with which the century was cursed, we were given to Formalism, Acmeism, Futurism, Modernism, Surrealism, Hyper-Realism, Dadaism, Dirty Realism,

Magic Realism and no doubt many more, all following Romanticism and Naturalism out of the nineteenth century and into the modern age. The isms are over – and writers fluctuate wildly as a result. Each movement had its credo (see **Manifesto**) and thought it had invented art and literature anew (see **Avant Garde**).

Itch

'When once the itch of literature comes over a man, nothing can cure it but the scratching of a pen.'

Samuel Lover

Ivory Towers

1 Hundreds and thousands of elephants were killed to provide homes for upper-class writers who had never been down a mine. Now, since brave efforts on the part of conservationists, writers live in bubbles, from which it is just as difficult to portray real life.

2 'Many will continue to think that art is a way of life for those who do not really live – a compensation or a surrogate. But this does

not justify any deliberate ivory tower: a poet must not turn his back on life. It is life which contrives to elude the poet.'

Eugenio Montale

Journalism

1 Described by Cyril Connolly (*Enemies of Promise*) as the Blue Bugloss – shiny, tempting and fatal to the serious artist, journalism is now generally more highly thought of and remunerated than literature.

2 'Journalists write because they have nothing to say, and have something to say because they write.'

Karl Kraus

Juvenilia

'I wanted to write like Dostoevsky.'

Sue Townsend

Kafka

'Am thinking of starting a movement to be called "Kafka Is Balls", with a club of which I propose to make myself Perpetual President. Not on the strength of having read Kafka – indeed I have never opened him – but because of what the highbrow magazines tell me about him. Am considering a button with the letters P.P.K.I.B.C. – Perpetual President Kafka Is Balls Club.'

James Agate

Kitchen Table

For women writers. It is comforting to (male) literary editors and reviewers (see *Women in Management in Publishing* [WIMP] for statistics showing extent of preponderance of men as editors and reviewers) to be able to dismiss a 'women's book' as something knocked off or whisked up in the proximity of the Magimix and the dishwasher. A homely dresser will, if possible, be included in the author's photo, complete with striped mugs and home-made bread.

Kitsch

'The feeling induced by kitsch must be a kind the multitudes can share. Kitsch may not, therefore, depend on an unusual situation; it must derive from the basic images people have engraved in their memories: the ungrateful daughter, the neglected father, children running on the grass, the motherland betrayed, first love.

Kitsch causes two tears to flow in quick succession. The first tear says: How nice to see children running on the grass!

The second tear says: How nice to be moved, together with all mankind, by children running on the grass!

It is the second tear that makes kitsch kitsch. The brotherhood of man on earth will be possible only on a base of kitsch.'

Milan Kundera

Language

1 'Language is the mother of thought, not its handmaiden.'

Karl Kraus

2 'It is language that tells us about the nature of a thing, provided that we respect language's own nature.'

Martin Heidegger

3 'Philosophical problems arise when language goes on holiday.'

Ludwig Wittgenstein

4 'Good writers are those who keep the language efficient. That is to say, keep it accurate, keep it clear. It doesn't matter whether the good writer wants to be useful, or whether the bad writer wants to do harm.'

Ezra Pound

Leavisite

A man (never a woman) who was taught and ineradicably influenced by F. R. Leavis – who was an admirer of Sir Clifford Chatterley's gamekeeper (see **Porn**).

Letters

'It has now become so much the fashion to publish letters, that in order to avoid it, I put as little into mine as I can.'

Samuel Johnson

Literary Agent

Asleep by day (see **Vampire**), literary agents take between 10 and 15 per cent of the author's advance and subsequent royalties, which they squander at night on booze and parties. (Estate agents take two and a half per cent. One way round the alarming discrepancy between what you must pay out when you sell your house and what is deducted at source when you sell your literary property is to ask an estate agent to sell your book for you. It is highly unlikely that a publisher will notice, provided the real estate Johnny has the good sense to invite him out to lunch.)

Many new writers think they will get nowhere unless they find an agent to represent them in the barracuda-infested pool of modern publishing. They fear, usually rightly, that an unsolicited manuscript will, on reaching the publisher, sink without trace (see **Slush Pile**).

The writer is advised to submit to a magazine, usually locally sponsored by an arts association, if the prospect of a literary agent seems unsatisfactory. There *are* people with a genuine interest in new writing, and they trawl small presses and magazines for new talent and promise.

Literary Festival

Fulfils the supremely English need to be rained on while making jokes like 'this is a fête worse than death'. With the fête, there are jumble stalls, donkey rides and a brass band; with the literary festival there is a jumble of (usually drunk) minor poets and fierce women handbagging those hapless locals who refer to them as 'Lady Novelist' or 'Poetess'. The brass band is replaced by the braying of the visiting Big Name. *'Dieu que le son du Burgess est triste au fond du bois!'* Many visit these sites for a view of Tom Paulin under tarpaulin or Imlah doing something simlah.

Literary Gentleman

1 A breed which until recently was almost extinct – but revived in the early years of

Thatcherism by the Young Fogey. Before this, the rise and fall of the Man of Letters could be detected in gentlemen's clubs (and in particular the Garrick) by the faint movement of a (tweed-clad) stomach under a copy of *The Times* (never the *TLS*, or even more common, a set of galley proofs in urgent need of attention: the Literary Gentleman preferred not to refer to his chosen profession in public).

The Literary Gentleman's favourite quotation was Anthony Powell's description of an undesirable personage: 'He was so wet you could shoot snipe off him.' This went well with the tweeds and suggested landed estates in the background.

Extreme misogyny is an essential part of the Man of Letters; and any woman who might have hoped, with the rise of feminism, to have found herself admitted to the Garrick in recognition of her literary endeavours was to be sorely disappointed. It seemed for a time that the Literary Gentleman had been caught unawares by the change in (publishing) methods. (He would on occasions be seen making his way to the site of a Georgian mansion in Bloomsbury, after lunch, apparently unaware that a large conglomerate had long ago swallowed him and his distinguished

Publishing House.) But the new breed more than compensates for the inadequacies of the old: assuming names drawn from the greatest in Eng. Lit., they still rule the Pages and the Waves.

2 'Literary men are a perpetual priesthood.'
Thomas Carlyle

Literary Novel

1 See **Remainder**. The beginning of the end: it was once assumed that most aspiring writers had literary ambitions, whether in the mode of Virginia Woolf or even J. B. Priestley. Now, so great is the commercialism of literature that the term 'literary novel', a revered form that contains a sneer within, had to be coined.

2 The Imperial Leather of the Book Trade. Can safely be taken to country house week-ends or visits to prospective in-laws – and is thoughtfully furnished with a large detach-able wrapper which can be placed over actual reading matter (see **Porn**).

Literary Widow

A thankless role and frequently far from the 'money for old mss' it is considered to be. The literary widow has to follow both the terms set out in a Will usually made by a terminally depressed/energetically crafty author who doesn't want his life written about for various good reasons and the demands of a public increasingly avid for personal and especially sexual detail of a famous writer. Ted Hughes and Sonia Orwell are supreme examples of the vilified relicts of authors – the issue is not so much whether what they did was 'right' or 'wrong' but that the insatiable appetite for salacious detail disguised by a strong moralistic tone makes monsters of anyone denying access to private papers and records, whether the late author would have sanctioned such access or not.

Literature

1 'The very essence of literature is the war between emotion and intellect, between life and death. When literature becomes too intellectual – when it begins to ignore the passions, the emotions – it becomes sterile,

silly, and actually without substance.'

Isaac Bashevis Singer

2 'The man of understanding can no more sit quiet and resigned while his country lets its literature decay, and lets good writing meet with contempt, than a good doctor could sit quiet and contented while some ignorant child was infecting itself with tuberculosis under the impression that it was merely eating jam tarts.'

Ezra Pound

3 'Literature flourishes best when it is half a trade and half an art.'

W. R. Inge

Little Magazine

Thin on the ground in England, better represented in America, the Little Magazine has lost readers and financial support in the face of relentless economic pressures. Once the seedbed of new talent, the Little Magazine has gone the way of the Rain Forest: why waste time finding out whether these really do provide oxygen when a quick buck can be made by felling trees and using them for publishing crap?

Log-Scratching

Sport of reviewers who band together to praise each others's books (see **Male Bonding**) and award prizes for who can roll over backwards fastest and who can make the best scratches on a log.

Loneliness

'I am sick of myself . . . My head aches. My heart – my hapless heart – is deluged in bitterness . . . I strive to study, I strive to write, but I cannot live without loving and being loved, without sympathy; if this is denied to me, I must die. Would that the hour were come!'

Journal of Mary Shelley

Lowbrow

1 Obs. See **Middlebrow; Highbrow**.

2 ' "I know it's not their fault, they haven't had the opportunity. But they're completely uninterested when those who *have* had opportunities attempt to show them things . . ."

"Perhaps one should be like everybody else," Gwen continued. "Simply tell them: 'Do this! Do that! Light the fire in the sitting-room! Lay the table! Make the bed! Then on your day off you can go and see the latest Hollywood crooner at the Majestic, followed by pastries and poached eggs at the Geisher cafe . . .' But it's all wrong! Can *nobody* help them?"

"Well, the borough councils are arranging these cultural cinemas and lectures we've been reading of," said Aron, to tease her.'

Julia Strachey (*An Integrated Many*)

Loyalty

Used to be demanded of an author by a publisher, but now the carousel goes round so fast the editor has jumped off or been pushed before the author can settle down to a small percentage and a sense of unrequited love. Star authors are particularly disloyal, and will leap for a lucrative deal, while dressing up the decision as loyalty to the new publisher (suddenly discovered to be a lifelong friend). See **Hubris**.

Lunch

1 A writer is not supposed to 'pitch' his or her book until the coffee, but extreme nervous-

ness and an unhealthy bank balance can lead to a diarrhoea of words before the arrival of the wine (a fatal mistake). As the final decision rests, these days, with other powers (see **Bookseller**) there is more chance of relaxing, however – should the assorted lunchers not prove too exhausting. These are usually literary agents taking a 'hair of the dog' before going to the office.

Wherever lunch may be held, it is important to look casual, but not to smell, if possible, as publishers have very sensitive olfactory organs (see **Wine**).

It is also important not to eat too fast, as this will give the impression of need. It must be borne in mind that the publisher has already eaten earlier in the day (see **Power Breakfast**) and the small portions he orders are because he is also looking forward to a party in the evening.

Do not leave the table to relieve yourself (and, of course, do not relieve yourself while at the table, either). Should you go away even for one moment, the man who holds the future in his hands will have been joined by a belfry of agents, all chirping over their latest find.

2 'I must say that luncheon was the limit. It

seemed to take one into a new and dreadful world. Can you imagine giving a lunch to celebrate the publication of a book? With other authors, mostly fairies, twittering all over the place, screaming "Oh Lionel!" and photographs of you holding the book, etc. Gosh! Dumas was the boy. When he had finished a novel he kept on sitting and started another. No snack luncheons for him.'

P. G. Wodehouse

Lunch Box

A parcel, or occasionally basket, of food left at the door of the writer who is a guest/prisoner in an Artists' Colony, and comprising generally bread, cheese and lettuce with optional apple. This attitude to the midday meal accounts for the worldwide absence of the Publisher's Colony.

Machismo

Writing is a sissy profession for a man. Unless fortunate enough to have a second string to your bow (see **Murderer**), the following proof that you're a bloke can be extremely useful: (a) bring all the Big Guns into your book – Shakespeare, Beethoven, etc. – and use important themes (see **Big Men's Books**); (b) write about children as though you knew about them.

Madness

1 A Russian reader of Gabriel Garcia Marquez's *One Hundred Years of Solitude*, a very old lady, was found copying out the whole novel, line by line, in her own hand. When asked why she was doing this she replied: 'Because I want to find out who is really mad, the author or me; and the only way to find out is to re-write the book.'

2 'The poet is in command of his fantasy, while it is exactly the mark of the neurotic that he is possessed by his fantasy.'

Lionel Trilling

Manifesto

A list of around ten commandments, usually printed in a periodical (see **Little Magazine**), which lays out the do's-and-don't's of a new movement (see **Avant-Garde**). There are no manifestos in our day because we are accustomed to rely on instructions on a Bran Flake packet for a guide to our mental health – and if we wish for more stimulating material, it comes free through the door.

Manners

The Novel of Manners involves working on Jane Austen's little piece of ivory and is therefore no longer an ecologically correct undertaking.

Marriage

1 'Can succeed for an artist only where there is enough money to save him from taking on uncongenial work and a wife who is intelligent and unselfish enough to understand and respect the working of the unfriendly cycle of the creative imagination. She will know at what point domestic happiness

begins to cloy, where love, tidiness, rent, rates, clothes, entertaining and rings at the doorbell should stop, and will recognise that there is no more sombre enemy of promise than the pram in the hall.'

Cyril Connolly

2 'Boy when I get to be 50 and if I'm famous, there will be no tributes to "the loving husband without whose help I would never have succeeded etc etc".'

Sylvia Plath

Masterpiece

'The true function of a writer is to produce a masterpiece and no other task is of any consequence.'

Cyril Connolly

Memory

'Literature transmits incontrovertible condensed experiences, from generation to generation. In this way literature becomes the living memory of a nation.'

Alexander Solzhenitsyn

Meteorology

'The poet may be used as the barometer, but let us not forget that he is also part of the weather.'

Lionel Trilling

Middlebrow

Once had connotations of chintzy sofa, a box of chocs and novel by J. B. Priestley or H. E. Bates. Most middlebrow people had a servant, and the servant would be expected to read a 'servants' novel', and to enjoy popular culture (see **Lowbrow**).

Mills and Boon

Written to a formula and therefore much admired by the Deconstructionists.

Misprints

'A poet can survive everything but a misprint.'

Oscar Wilde

Modernism

Considered by those taking advantage of the present cultural climate (see **New Barbarian**) to have been invented by an intellectual élite in order to confuse and depress the masses – who, quite rightly, don't know much about art but know what they like (see **Good Read**). To believe this is to go down the primrose path to the everlasting hot-water-bottle.

Money

1 'No man but a blockhead ever wrote except for money.'

Samuel Johnson

2 'The impulse to create beauty is rather rare in literary men . . . Far ahead comes the yearning to make money. And after the yearning to make money comes the yearning to make noise.'

H. L. Mencken

Murder All Your Little Darlings

Well worn advice to the writer: go over what you have written, find the passages which are nearest to your heart – and CUT THEM OUT!

Murderer

If you can't actually be one, it can be profitable to befriend one and write about his appalling crime (Mailer; Truman Capote).

The main problem for the writer is in creating an interesting enough murderer, when the character is drawn from real life. Most brutal killers are dull company and efforts on the part of their 'authors' to bring them to life on the page end up more deadly than the Gas Chamber.

Queens of Crime such as Ruth Rendell, her *alter ego* Barbara Vine and Patricia Highsmith know how to describe a murderer: not the Romantic anti-hero as portrayed by the faction writers – a Frankenstein's Monster, the Dracula of the Country Club – but a chilling picture of the psychotic male.

Names

'Choosing names is one of the novelist's bug-bears. A character will not answer to the wrong name. I like Dickensian names of the Tulkinghorn type, and do not object to those that are directly descriptive like Overreach or Sneerwell.'

L. P. Hartley

Narrator

In the days of Empire, the Narrator was omniscient: he (invariably a he) knew everything, just as he owned everything. The best example of the 'Unreliable Narrator' came form Ford Madox Ford's *The Good Soldier*, just as the First World War took away all the certainties.

New Barbarian

A writer who can write only schlock and goes to great lengths to expound the new philosophy: if it's popular it's good, if it's not it's bad, therefore as I am popular I am the good new thing. This type of writer can develop Hitlerian tendencies and will even go as far as to produce a 'Review' and write a column; and is often seen stroking a fluffy cat, in the shape of one subtle, literary but unpopular writer.

New Book

'When a new book is published, read an old one.'

Samuel Rogers

New Fiction

A despised category in these days of Mega Sales from Madonna fictionalizing herself and multiple Marilyns. One editor, Liz Calder, stands out in British publishing as a tireless champion of the promising, the new and untried. Her publishing company Bloomsbury should not be confused with the **Bloomsbury Group**, which now stands for everything that is stale, over-exploited and dated.

New Technology

'The sad thing about artificial intelligence is that it lacks artifice and therefore intelligence.'

Jean Baudrillard

News

'Literature is news that STAYS news.'

Ezra Pound

Niche

A publisher's term for the Chamber of Horrors; authors in this category find their book has been hung on a 'peg' or 'handle' and is left there to die in the dark.

Novel

1 'The novel is not a suitable form for young writers. The best novels (of Stendhal, Flaubert, Proust, James, etc.) are written from early middle age onwards.'

Cyril Connolly

2 'To write a novel may be pure pleasure. To live a novel presents certain difficulties. As for reading a novel, I do my best to get out of it.'

Karl Kraus

3 'Perhaps we have had too many novels. People no longer seem to need them. On the other hand, pictorial biographies – real pictures of real lives – exist in abundance, and

there will be more of these in the coming years. The camera is ubiquitous.'

Leon Edel

O, Story of

French Porn. Hard to blow and ultimately unsatisfactory.

Oatmeal

'We cultivate literature on a little oatmeal.'
Sydney Smith, proposing a motto
for the Edinburgh Review

Objectivity

'To chemists there is nothing unclean in this world. A man of letters should be as objective as a chemist; he has to renounce ordinary subjectivity and realize that manure piles play a very respectable role in a landscape and that evil passions are as inherent in life as good ones.'

Anton Chekhov

Obsession

'Obsession begets poems. But you need to vary your obsessions. One obsession, one poem. There was a Victorian poet, A. J. Munby, a disciple of Browning's, and not a

bad versifier altogether, who was obsessed by
servant girls and a desire to sleep with them,
if they were beautiful enough. Marrying such
a girl, "built for beauty, indeed, but certainly
built for labour", did justice to her beauty
(Munby was a Christian Socialist) and proved
a moral superiority to class distinction. Red
hands and arms red to the elbow from the
sink were an obsession within his obsession;
which produced a monotony in his poems.
Munby did marry his cook, a sensible girl who
preferred to live below stairs by day and to act
Mrs Munby only in the secrecy of night.'

Geoffrey Grigson

Oedipus Complex

1 'This won't explain everything, nor even
the *Oedipus*.'

Louis MacNeice

2 'Death of the Father would deprive literature of many of its pleasures. If there is no
longer a Father, why tell stories? Doesn't
every narrative lead back to Oedipus? Isn't
storytelling always a way of searching for
one's origin?'

Roland Barthes

Old Wives' Tale

'There is something of an old wives' tale in fine literature.'

W. B. Yeats

One

'In fact, reading Calvino, I had the unnerving sense that I was also writing what he had written; thus does his art prove his case as writer and reader become one, or One.'

Gore Vidal

Opium

It is a mistake to believe that the taking of drugs facilitates the creative process. Samuel Taylor Coleridge was fortunate to be visited in his opium stupor in Somerset by a person who wrote 'Kubla Khan' and then tiptoed away back to Porlock.

Option

Good books are ruined by being made into a film. Producers offer 10 per cent of the sum payable in the (highly improbable) event of the film's being made. Advice to writers: cut and run.

Oral Tradition

What you heard at your mother's knee. The Grimm Brothers went to the source of all told fairy-tales and picked out only those where the lad is brave and strong and the lass weak and helpless. This is responsible for most of the trouble in the world ever since.

Orwell

He's already thought what you've just thought.

Paperback Original

Reduces the status of the author from grande to petite horizontale.

Paperback Revolution

The publishing of books straight into paperback (as in France) is promised here every few years, but, like the abolition of the House of Lords, never takes place.

Parenthood

'I feel rather paternal tenderness (towards my early books), the same thing you feel for children who have grown up and left home. I see those early books as far away and defenceless and remember all the headaches they gave the young man who wrote them.'

Gabriel Garcia Marquez

Pension

Writers are not in line for pensions and are financially secure only if their books don't retire before them.

Perfection

'The perfect poem – freshness of cadence, picture, sense and proportion, salted by a
deliberate break or breaks in its perfection.
Yes, but who has written it?'

Geoffrey Grigson

Personality

'The great mischief has always been that
whenever our reviewers deviate from the
usual and popular course of panegyric, they
start from and end in personality, so that the
public mind is almost sure to connect
unfavourable criticism with personal ani-
mosity.'

E. L. Godkin

Philistine

(One who) 'is habitually bored and looks for
things that won't bore him. An artist finds
things boring, but is never bored.'

Karl Kraus

Photo-Realism

A part of the wild rush into fragmentation and chaos which characterizes the present climate in American – and British – fiction. Trendy categorization abounds: experimental realism, hyper realism, critical realism, fantastic realism, magic realism, dirty realism and so on. These 'schools' are created in order to spread panic and gloom and keep a clique in the news (see **Log-Rolling**). The best antidote is to go to a performance of *Love Labour's Lost*.

Pinteresque

An irritating way of describing a pause.

Piracy

Fredrick Forsyth, in Urdu.

Pitch

Hollywood screenwriters are capable of pitching storylines and ideas (see **Concept**) at a rate of two hundred a day. As it is impossible to compete with this, aspiring screenwriters are advised to take the plot of a famous classic, e.g. *A Midsummer Night's Dream*, and update it (*Tit Falls for Ass*) and wait for the studio mogul's delighted reaction (*Dustin's my Bottom*).

Plagiarism

1 A pact struck between two writers – one unknown, or at least way past his prime – and an up-and-coming, prize-hungry scribbler. The deal goes like this: in return for taking plot, characters and main story line from the publicity-defunct writer, the young Turk discreetly organizes a 'leak' revealing the disgraceful theft of a work by another author. The resulting headlines and investigative articles ensure sales and multi-media attention for the ambitious young writer, while the older and forgotten originator of the book can at best look forward to another lease of life (see **Discovered Writer**) or at least rest contented with a posthumous existence as a footnote in the Halls of Fame. Warning to the aspiring plagiarist: the whole thing can backfire badly, and result in a court case, fine or prison sentence, and destruction of the novel on which all hopes rested (see **Pulp**).

2 'Immature poets imitate; mature poets steal.'

T. S. Eliot

3 'A Plagiarist should be made to copy the author a hundred times.'

Karl Kraus

Plan

'Of course, if he did plan the whole thing out first, there is nothing so very bizarre in the idea of writing so many hundred words of it each day. After all, it is more or less what one does oneself. One sits down to work each morning, no matter whether one feels bright or lethargic, and before one gets up a certain amount of stuff, generally about fifteen hundred words, has emerged.'

P. G. Wodehouse, on Trollope

Player

When the deal becomes more important than the work of literature involved, publishers like to think of themselves as Players (see **Power Breakfast**). Even though there is another meal to look forward to in the near future (see **Lunch**), most publishers would rather be

Players than Gentlemen and few books that are not worth a Deal get published at all.

Poetry

1 'Searches for the melody of nature in the noise of a dictionary.'

Boris Pasternak

2 'Poetry is the most difficult of the arts.'

Paul Valery

3 'Well, if this is poetry, it is very easy to write.'

William Morris

Poison

'Some sentences release their poison only after years.'

Elias Canetti

Political Correctness

Fortunes to be made from attacking it (see Camilla Paglia).

Politics

1 'A great writer is, so to speak, a second government in his country. And for that reason no regime has ever loved great writers, only minor ones.'

Alexander Solzhenitsyn

2 (Politics) 'are more dangerous to young writers than journalism. They are dangerous because writers now feel that politics are necessary to them, without having learnt how best to be political.'

Cyril Connolly

Porn

Invented by Sir Clifford Chatterley, an invalid with a large country seat who asked his game-keeper Mellors to ease the strain in Sir Clifford's marital relations with his wife Connie. The ensuing – and embarrassing – consequence of this request, once committed to paper by the author D. H. Lawrence, was considered improper reading by those in charge of the nation's Moral Outlook and the book was banned. (For a time the more whimsical amongst the literati referred to their private parts as John Thomas and Lady Jane;

no gamekeeper, however, was known to follow this fad.)

All this led to a court case in 1963 where the book, *Lady Chatterley's Lover*, was deemed not to be Porn – which, of course, established it as such in perpetuity and brought great riches to its publishers.

The lifting of censorship might be though to have led to a great flowering of Porn from the pens of those gifted writers hitherto denied freedom of expression in penetrating the mysteries and moral significance of the sexual act. This has not been the case and Porn has now degenerated into a web of groups and counter groups, such as *Feminists Against Women Against Porn, Women Against Censorship Against Women*, etc. Not recommended for a new writer, however exciting the gimmick may be (Telephone Sex, Sex in Virtual Reality, and so on).

Portion and Outline

Many writers present an outline for a book, along with a couple of chapters, in order to secure an advance. These embryonic pieces of writing often remain just that. Advice to the writer who has spawned several of them is to stick them all together, send them as a novel by a cousin of Italo Calvino in a foreign-looking envelope to Faber & Faber, and emigrate.

Post-Modernism

A mix and mis-match of styles, times, tenses, etc., in the novel. As difficult to define as to read – and certainly not worth the attention of the novice writer as now out of date.

Post-Post Modernism

Sticking it all together again. Attempt on the part of the serious writer to return to the old form of the novel, i.e. plot, linear narrative, development of character, etc. In fact a desperate try for a wider readership without losing dignity.

Posterity

1 'Really the writer doesn't want success. He knows he has a short span of life, that the day will come when he must pass through the wall of oblivion, and he wants to leave a scratch on the wall – Kilroy was here – that somebody a hundred, or a thousand years later will see.'
William Faulkner

2 'I am quite content to go down to posterity as a scissors and paste man for that seems to me a harsh but not unjust description.'

James Joyce, alluding to the composition
of *Finnegan's Wake*

3 'Trying to make your poems lick the arse of posterity is as bad as making them lick the arse of your own time. Either way you twist their truth to yourself – unless hindquarters are your natural habitat.'

Geoffrey Grigson

4 **Posterity, writing for**. A genteel way for a writer to describe being on the dole.

Potboiler

1 obs. Belongs to the age of highbrow, middlebrow, etc., when a serious literary figure could say with a shame-faced laugh that he was 'tossing off' a potboiler in order to pay the bills while concentrating in reality on Higher Things. Every book must boil the publisher's pot these days, let alone the author's, and no writer is expected to be thinking at any time of Higher Things.

2 'I think this piece will help the pot boil.'

John Wolcot (first use of 'potboiler', c. 1790)

3 'To write a pot boiler, that is genius.

Charles Baudelaire

Power Breakfast

Pathetic attempt on the part of the publisher to emulate Hollywood. Venue: a swanky hotel. Usually for transatlantic deals – where the Americans are disgusted by British coffee and vice versa. The writer is never invited.

Pram in the Hall

See **Marriage**.

Prizes

'Every poet looks down on prizes, until he is given a prize. Then he recovers from this affront to himself and continues to look down on prizes. Rightly.'

Geoffrey Grigson

Professional Writer

(One who) 'labours in the first place for food, shelter, tailors, a woman, European travel, horses, stalls at the opera, good cigars, ambrosial evenings in restaurants; and gives glory the best chance he can.'

Arnold Bennett

Provinces

Heavily populated by writers and would-be writers who think (rightly) that the Capital is a hive of cliques with no intention whatsoever of paying the slightest notice to the provincial literary person. These blighted individuals have two methods of redress (see **Literary Festival; Revenge**).

Pseudonym

Used by popular prolific writers who switch genre – 'History' to 'Romantic' and back again – and (a now dying practice) by dons who write detective novels. Only the Portuguese poet Pessoa genuinely had so many voices and personalities that 'heteronyms' running into double figures were needed. A striking example of the failure of a pseudonym was Doris Lessing's adoption of the name 'Jane Somers' in order to prove that she was only reviewed because everyone knew who she was. Jane Somers duly went unnoticed, but it was impossible to prove that the reason for this was literary élitism rather than a genuine lack on interest in the book.

PTQ

Page Turning Quality. For those caught short in the Bush.

Publisher

1 Most common illnesses: *folie de grandeur*; dyspepsia. Most usual form of clothing: tweeds (see **Literary Gentleman**); black polo-neck (see **Pinter Imitation**); caftan (see **New Age**); velvet plus fours (see **Sissinghurst**).

2 'It took me five years to find a publisher.'
Gabriel Garcia Marquez

Publisher's Party

Hype springs eternal.

Pulp

1 Originally a publication printed on rough paper made from wood-pulp, often containing sensational or poor-quality writing.

2 Final expression of disgust by a publisher at a book ingested by the company which has got stuck in the works, refuses to 'go well' and is in need of shredding to save the health of the organization.

Pulpit

'I think it an abuse to use the novel as a pulpit or a platform, and I believe readers are misguided when they suppose they can thus easily acquire knowledge.'

W. Somerset Maugham

Punctuation

'I once left a publisher for the sole reason that he tried to change my semicolons to periods.'

Milan Kundera

Purpose

'If he wrote it he could get rid of it. He had gotten rid of many things by writing them.'

Ernest Hemingway

Qualms, Lack of

1 'No author ever spared a brother.'

John Gay

2 'Writers are always selling somebody out.'

Joan Didion

3 'The writer's only responsibility is to his art. He will be completely ruthless if he is a good one . . . If a writer has to rob his mother he will not hesitate; the *Ode to a Grecian Urn* is worth any number of old ladies.'

William Faulkner

Quantity

1 'The more a man writes, the more he can write.'

William Hazlitt

2 'The poets who are not prolific, who write cautiously but seldom badly, miss both the failures and the triumphs. The triumphs come from those bursting prolific poets who don't give a damn if they are writing well or badly. A bad poet is one who always writes badly.'

Geoffrey Grigson

Quarrel

'We make out of the quarrel with others, rhetoric, but of the quarrel with ourselves, poetry.'

W. B. Yeats

Quest Novel

Why is it so boring?

Reader

1 'Most readers live in London; they are run-down, querulous, constipated, soot-ridden, stained with asphalt and nicotine and, as a result of sitting all day in a chair in a box and eating too fast, slightly mad sufferers from indigestion.'

Cyril Connolly

2 'Unless a reader is able to give something of himself, he cannot get from a novel the best it has to give.'

W. Somerset Maugham

3 **Reader, Publishers'**. Harassed, underpaid mother (or father) of triplets trying to earn a bit on the side by reading manuscripts and pronouncing on them.

Reader's Report

Incoherent, often smudged with wine, babies' excrement and other effluvia from the home of the Publisher's Reader. The author's life and future depends on the sleepless night suffered by the Reader and her/his brood.

Reading

1 'How little you have read, how little you know; but your random reading determines what you are.'

Elias Canetti

2 'It is strange that there should be so little reading in the world, and so much writing. People in general do not willingly read, if they can have any thing else to amuse them.'

Samuel Johnson

Redundancies

Ethnic cleansing carried out by Conglomerates.

Rejection

1 Retype title page and submit elsewhere (after removing the hair placed on page 30).

2 Famous cases of a novel rejected which then turns out to be of seminal importance are *Animal Farm* by George Orwell, rejected by Faber; and *Lord of the Flies* by William Golding, rejected by everyone *except* Faber, who saw the reason was an unreadable first chapter

(this was later removed). John Kennedy Toole's *A Confederacy of Dunces* suffered multiple rejections which led the author to an early suicide; his mother touted the manuscript around until it was taken and her son's gifts recognized. Samuel Beckett was also much rejected with his first novel *Murphy*. It is important that rejection should not lead to permanent dejection. It is usually better to start again than to give up – or insist on going it alone (see **Vanity Publishing**).

3 'A good many young writers make the mistake of enclosing a stamped, self-addressed envelope, big enough for the manuscript to come back in. This is too much of a temptation to the editor.'

Ring Lardner

Remainder

Books published in hard cover which have begun to bore and irritate the publisher. These are sold off cheap and can be found in the most insalubrious places, including baskets on pavements outside the portals of bookshops. Advice to the Writer: buy up as many of these as you can afford and create an 'antiquarian corner' in your home in which they are given a prominent position. Tell your friends you are visited on a regular basis by rare book dealers and are considering offers on your 'Modern First Editions'.

Rep

A travelling salesman who must make the best of the publisher's wares – e.g. 'This is a snazzy, sexy why-dunnit with new revelations about Marilyn Monroe.'

Reputation

It is by now virtually impossible for a publisher to develop an author's talent and ability by showing faith and publishing that author's first, second and third novel with the quiet confidence that one day that author's reprints will follow. Reputations are made through magazine interviews and TV appearances (see **Interview**). Fall once and you're likely to stay there – unless you can come up quick with a book about a serial killer taping Princess Diana.

Research

'The greatest part of a writer's time is spent in reading, in order to write; a man will turn over half a library to write one book.'

Samuel Johnson

Returns

A book goes out in party dress to the big, bright store and comes back unsold. Neither the publisher nor the author can do anything about this – but a recent trend, known as 'Firm Sale', whereby the bookseller orders an unreturnable quantity of the book, may mean the party will soon be attended only by Barbara Taylor Bradford and Jeffrey Archer.

Revenge

The most daring act of retribution on the part of an author whose calls were never returned was enacted by an American scribe, who rented a plane and buzzed his publisher's skyscraper, while the terrified CEO and MD cowered under their desks, and was rewarded with massive sales as a result of the ensuing publicity. Other authors have threatened to throw acid and other noxious substances into their publisher's offices – but most who feel themselves eternally slighted retire to a cold, unsanitary hovel in an isolated rural spot and pass the time with a bottle until the call comes that will awaken them from the dead (see **Discovered Writer**).

Reviewers

1 'Too often do reviewers remind us of the mob of Astrologers, Chaldeans and Sooth-sayers gathered before the "writing on the wall" and unable to read the characters or make known the interpretation.'

Charlotte Brontë

2 'It is impossible for a [woman] to say to them this book is bad, this picture is feeble, or whatever it may be, without giving far more pain and rousing far more anger than a man would who gave the same criticism.'

Virginia Woolf

3 **Reviewer's Adjectives.** 'Beautifully written' – Won't sell a copy. 'Nabokovian' – Tricksy. 'Proustian' – The book has something about memory in it. 'Rabelaisian' – The book has some dirty jokes in it.

Revision

1 'Too much polishing weakens rather than improves a work.'

Pliny the Younger

2 'If life had a second edition, how I would correct the proofs.'

John Clare

Roman à Clef

Novel in which the characters are recognizably drawn from real life. Lafayette's *La Princesse de Clèves* was the first.

Note to writer: if you must risk trouble, there is no point believing that employing the words 'all characters in this book are fictitious and bear no resemblance . . .' will make any difference whatsoever. One trick is to mention by his or her actual name a very minor character in the book and then go to town with a fictitious character who has all the ridiculous personality disorders you wish to delineate. 'It can't be Donald Trump because he is mentioned in the book by name,' cries the naïve reader. None of this really stands up in court.

Royalties

Paid occasionally (sometimes never) by publishers, but always in arrears, so as to give the publisher at least six month's interest on money owed to the author. The 'balance sheet' is sent to the author, who is unable to decipher it – or to obtain elucidation from his or her agent, who is equally baffled by the arcane accounting system.

S

Samizdat

Once an underground press printing stories and poetry by dissidents in the USSR and Eastern Bloc. Now extinct: writers from all over have to depend on the tender mercies of publishers and literary agents.

Science Fiction

The great days of SF are over. The genre – which depended on the technological revolution to spark off its most fertile creators (Outer Space, Robotic Intelligences, etc.) took an interesting leap sideways with the work of J. G. Ballard (see **Inner Space**) and now is at its most fruitful in the hands of women: Margaret Atwood (*The Handmaid's Tale*), Marge Piercy and Ursula le Guin.

Schlock

A work in which not one aspect has any truth: the characters are wooden and behave as puppets in a marionette show run by an advertising company (Sex and Shopping); the settings are rich and improbable (Penthouse, Palm-fringed beach); and the plot culminates in 'success' (Money). Writers of Schlock go neither to Hell nor Purgatory but to unending Bimbo.

Screenplay

1 Should be 120 pages in length and should never contain the line 'Where's Dave?'

2 The moving finger writes and having writ, rewrites and rewrites again. Those contemplating writing a screenplay must resign themselves to the end product bearing no resemblance whatsoever to the original draft. Illnesses and nervous breakdowns which result from these incessant changes are treated by a Script Doctor, who usually amputates.

Script

Basic ingredients for success: sex scenes to which gays/lesbians/hermaphrodites can object publicly; violence, committed if possible by a bisexual serial killer with a background of childhood abuse.

Self-Deprecation

'Among authors [self-deprecation] never rings true. Why publish a work at all if you think it's no good? (Unless it's a potboiler, in which case say so.)'

Louis MacNeice

Sex

1 The aspiring writer is inclined (if male) to start a novel with a scene of masturbation. This is nearly always a mistake. Sex – of any kind – is notoriously difficult to write about and even the most practised and gifted of writers are guilty of producing passages which, if summarized, say no more than 'he had his way with her' or 'he had his way with him' or 'she had her way' etc. Recommended reading: Stendhal's *De L'Amour* and *A Lover's Discourse* by Roland Barthes. The French are interested in sex and the English prefer to talk about the weather – a cliché which still holds true after Lady Chatterley *et al*.

2 'The charlock of wild mustard throws a more baleful shade on the young shoot when it is the love that dare not speak its name.'

Cyril Connolly

3 'The more a man cultivates the arts the less he fornicates.'

Charles Baudelaire

Shit

'Shit has its own integrity.' (Hollywood scriptwriters' axiom)

Sissinghurst

House in Kent, an important component of English literary history (see **Heritage**) where the famous aristocrat and gardener Vita Sackville-West had an affair with Virginia Woolf (see **Bloomsbury Group**). Renowned for its 'white garden', Sissinghurst now houses an eminent Literary Agent who entertains on the third Sunday of every month in full Vita gear – riding habit, monogrammed linen shirt – for the benefit of overseas publishers.

Skipping

1 'The wise reader will get the greatest enjoyment out of reading literature if he learns the useful art of skipping ... but to

skip without loss is not easy.'

W. Somerset Maugham

2 'Dr Johnson had a peculiar facility in seizing at once what was valuable in any book without submitting to the labour of perusing it from beginning to end.'

Boswell

Sleep

'The best way to understand James Joyce's method is to note what goes on in one's own mind when one is just dropping off to sleep.'

Edmund Wilson

Small Publishers

Pet food (see **Conglomerates**); rapidly swallowed and frequently regurgitated.

Stream of Consciousness

See **El Vino's**.

Structure

1 'As in all my books for a long time the problem was structure. I never start writing until I've sorted that out.'

Gabriel Garcia Marquez

2 'If a writer omits something because he does not know it, then there is a hole in the story.'

Ernest Hemingway

Style

1 'The true writer has nothing to say. What counts is the way he says it.'

Alain Robbe-Gillet

2 'What seems beautiful to me, what I should like to write, is a book about nothing, a book dependent on nothing external, which would be held together by the internal strength of its style, just as the earth, suspended in the void, depends on nothing external for its support; a book which would have almost no subject, or at least in which the subject would be almost invisible, if such a thing is possible. The finest works are those that contain the least matter; the closer language comes to thought, the

closer language comes to coinciding and merging with it, the finer the result.'

Gustave Flaubert

3 'Writing, when properly managed, is but a different name for conversation.'

Laurence Sterne

Subjects

Not to write about: concentration camps, Sylvia Plath, post-modernist versions of Little Red Riding Hood.

Success

1 'Success is a poison that should only be taken late in life, then only in small doses.'

Trollope

2 'Of all the enemies of literature, success is the most insidious.'

Cyril Connolly

Success, Recipes for

1 'Make 'em laugh; make 'em cry; make 'em wait.'

Charles Reade

2 'A writer can go far if he combines a certain talent for dramatization and a facility for speaking everyone's language, with the art of exploiting the passions of the day, the concerns of the moment.'

Gustave Flaubert

Surrealism

Increasingly impossible to write in this vein, in an increasingly surreal world. Dada for the ga-ga.

Synergy

Tie-jobs for the Big Ones: TV, film, mini-series paperbacks (at least three) of same book but with different prices and covers. Floating debris for Outer Space.

Syntax

The study of how the items of a language, independent of their semantics, can be combined or decomposed. In languages it specifies a set of grammatical categories and a set of rules which define the ways in which larger items are built up from smaller units.

Takeover

A huge conglomerate swallows a small, 'dignified' publishing house. An interesting subject to write about if a member of the **Brat Pack**, as the money on offer will change radically (see **Advance**; **Lunch**) and a description of the long-dead Eighties when this sort of thing took place can be compared to Scott Fitzgerald. Advice to writer: always check, when sending out mss, that all the publishers to whom you are offering your precious life's work are not under the same umbrella. A considerable saving on postage can accrue here – for if one of the group says 'no' (see **Rejection**), it's highly likely the others will say the same. The reason? All share the same paperback division, and without paperback (which will already have turned your book down on the first showing) your book will not be 'viable'.

Talent

'It took me fifteen years to discover that I had no talent for writing; but I couldn't give it up because by that time I was too famous.'

Robert Benchley

Teeth

1 'Dialectics, a kind of false teeth.'

Elias Canetti

2 'Writers, like teeth, are divided into incisors and grinders.'

Walter Bagehot

Television

'The TV: every image is an ephemeral vanishing act. But art is the same. In its countless contemporary forms, its only magic is the magic of disappearance, and the pleasures it gives are bloodless ones.'

Jean Baudrillard

Text

According to the French, writes itself without aid of an author. See **Automatic Writing**.

Theories

1 'I am always suspicious of a novelist's theories; I have never known them to be any-

thing other than a justification for his own shortcomings.'

W. Somerset Maugham

2 'My whole theory of writing I can sum up in one sentence. An author ought to write for the youth of his own generation, the critics of the next, and the schoolmasters of ever afterward.'

F. Scott Fitzgerald

Tour de Force

Term used when the reviewer doesn't know what to say about a novel by a relative of a friend.

Tragedy

'Show me a hero and I will write you a tragedy.'

F. Scott Fitzgerald

Translations

'Some hold translations not to be unlike the wrong side of a Turkey tapestry.'

James Howell

Typewriter

'The famous gesture of tearing one's page from the typewriter, by which writers or journalists elevate themselves to the status of Wild West heroes drawing their six-shooters.'

Jean Baudrillard

Unlikeable

'Unlikeable in life; likeable in literature.'

V. S. Pritchett

USP (Unique Selling Point)

Invented in the early Eighties, USP came about as a result of growing market pressures: no longer able to write a novel that wasn't actually *about* anything, writers were advised to pick on a Selling Point. This would provide suitable remuneration from the publisher (see **Advance**) and sell to the public as well – which turned out to be a more questionable matter (see **Returns**). Many chose Big Themes, such as Roots, Nationality and Race; others chose The Globe. Long wearisome journeys (for the white male) became a necessity. Much of the need for the USP came from the galling fact that women and members of ethnic minorities were finding their voice as never before – their USP had no need to be invented.

Values

'Literature is, to my mind, the great teaching power of the world, the ultimate creator of all values . . . It must take the responsibility of its power and keep its freedom.'

W. B. Yeats

Vanity Publishing

The writer pays to have his/her work made into a book. This was always the practice in the days before the publisher invested in the writer; and in the case of Robert Burns led to the plangent poem 'Willie's Awa'', written from Edinburgh when Burns's printer Willie took the sovereigns for a new book of poems and rushed south to enjoy the fleshpots of London. Vanity publishers today should be carefully vetted in case they're found on the Costa Brava just when you thought your tome was about to hit the bookstalls.

Verisimilitude

'Verisimilitude is a rare quality in English literature. Defoe achieved it and so did Jane Austen, and Scott in one or two of his short stories ... (it) is not the same as realism, whose great weakness is that it is arbitrary: we see the novelist choosing this and that as "real": but verisimilitude works to a stricter limitation, going for the skin, the surface of things, and arguing that if we know the skin we can fill in what is beneath it from our own knowledge of the world.'

V. S. Pritchett

Virgina Woolf

Well marketed but little read – a 'difficult' writer who would have been surprised to find herself a part of the Biography Trade's dream and thus a leading light of the Eng. Lit. Tourist Industry (see **Heritage**). It is presumably only a question of time before *To The Lighthouse* is printed on tea towels and a statue to the coterie to which she and her sister Vanessa Bell belonged takes pride of place in Bedford Square (see **Bloomsbury Group**).

Virtue

'Reading maketh a full man, conference a ready man, and writing an exact man.'

Francis Bacon

Vulgarity

'Fear of [vulgarity] can be as vulgar as anything. Just as a wing three-quarter who's to score in Rugby football must generally hug the touch-line, so creative literature, which by its nature involves personal feelings, must run the risk of sentimentality. But it's better to be sometimes sentimental, over-clouded, hyperbolical or merely obvious than to play for safety always and get nowhere. Virgil, Shakespeare, Dickens and countless others were thrust into touch in their time.'

Louis MacNeice

What's It Like?

Question asked by the publisher when told of a book by a new, unheard-of writer. Suitable answers: *The Naked and the Dead*, seen through the eyes of a woman; a downmarket *Gone With The Wind* set in East Sussex.

Wine

1 If offered by publisher in his office, be prepared for Gnat's Piss.

2 A publisher will take great care choosing his vintage claret when he is the guest of another publisher. The waiter will know that the situation is very different when the same publisher is host, and has seen him order accordingly: Perrier for poetry; plonk for prose; Chateau-Yquem for schlock; and a jeroboam for Jeffrey Archer.

Women Writers

1 As pointed out by the innovative writer Christine Brooke-Rose, women writers are expected either to imitate men or to write about their lives (see **Kitchen Table**).

2 'In dealing with women as writers, as much elasticity as possible is desirable; it is necessary to leave oneself room to deal with other things beside their work, so much has work been influenced by conditions having nothing whatever to do with art.'

Virgina Woolf

Word Processor

A machine which produces long, repetitive, meandering novels. The Writer, bemused by the screen and the endless possibility of adding material, forgets to subtract. Many hitherto unassailable reputations have been wrecked by the word processor and by the ignoring of Ford Madox Ford's maxim, WHEN IN DOUBT, CUT.

Words

'In the dark, words weigh double.'

Elias Canetti

Work

1 'That dry drudgery at desk's dead wood.'

Charles Lamb

2 'Never in my life have I written anything more difficult than what I am doing now – trivial dialogue. This inn scene will perhaps take me three months, I can't tell. There are moments when I want to weep, I feel so powerless. But I'll die rather than botch it.'

Gustave Flaubert

Writer

1 'Every writer would like to push the next writer into the past and feel sorry for him there.'

Elias Canetti

2 'A writer is like a bean plant – he has his little day, and then he gets stringy.'

Elwyn Brooks White

3 'The ablest writer is a gardener first, and then a cook. His tasks are, carefully to select and cultivate his strongest and most nutritive thoughts, and, when they are ripe, to dress them wholesomely, and so that they might have a relish.'

J. C. and A. W. Hare

Writing

1 'If I were to be taken beyond the ocean, into Paradise, and forbidden to write, I would refuse the ocean and the Paradise.'

Marina Tsvetayeva

2 'I am convinced more and more day by day that fine writing is next to fine doing, the top thing in the world.'

John Keats

3 'It has to be said that writing is an inhuman and unintelligible activity – one must always do it with a certain disdain, without illusions, and leave it to others to believe in one's own work.'

Jean Baudrillard

Wylie

Comes before **Writing**.

Xenophobia

See **Hampstead Novel**.

Yeti

Comes in and out of fashion cyclically, depending on the value of the yen.

Zed

'In language there is a spice of spelling. So I fancy a Society for the Defence of the Letter Zed. The verbs which end in -*ize*, which the house-styles of unfeeling publishers, lazy printers, and newspapers smooth into -*ise*. Zenith. Zedoary. Adze. Azimuth, Zodiac, strongholds of Zed.'

Geoffrey Grigson

Zen

The art of neither writing nor reading.